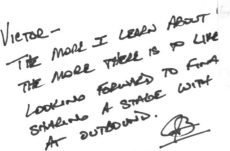

Victor—
The more I learn about
the more there is to like
Looking forward to find
sharing a stage with
at outbound.

# WHEN IT GOES

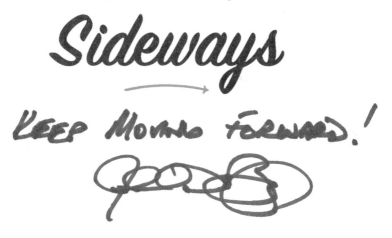

## Sideways

Keep Moving Forward!

---

by Jeff Bajorek
jeffbajorek.com

Illustration and design by Liz Borchert
llbd.co

Marketing and production by Slabtown Marketing
slabtownmarketing.com

Keep Moving Forward!

RETHINK THE $ WAY YOU SELL

# Introduction

**M**ama told me there'd be days like this...

The spring of 2020 has been interesting to say the least. We've got a global pandemic on our hands, the likes of which most of us have never seen in our lifetimes, and those of us who've lived through the last one weren't old enough then to remember it.

A lot of salespeople have been genuinely perplexed by the situation and what to do.

*"Should I keep selling?"*

*"I don't want to appear tone deaf..."*

*"I feel like I should be doing something..."*

*"What do I say?"*

The more I've thought about approaching the situation, the more I realize it presents similar challenges to other times in my career when the chips have been down. In sales, we're used to regular ups and downs, but the closest thing I can compare this situation to is the economic downturn of 2008-09. There was a ton of uncertainty then, as there is now, but a lot of people sold very successfully all the way through it, because they were able to focus on what really mattered.

What mattered then still matters now.

Whether it's a global pandemic, an economic downturn, tough times for your company or just a personal slump for you, it's important not to panic. Instead, reflect on what got you here, what was in your control, what wasn't, and what you can control moving forward to get out of it.

I put this guide together to highlight and remind you of the fundamentals that are necessary in times like these. Interestingly enough, these are the same principles that will help you succeed in any climate at any time. This may be your first, but it will most certainly not be the last time there is uncertainty in your marketplace during your career.

Consider this a reference to ground you during those times, and a roadmap for the best way to sell during challenging seasons. I've experienced dips in my career, and these are the strategies that helped me get through those ruts and beyond them.

Be patient and remember that this too shall pass. There's always a lesson in adversity, and an opportunity to grow if you're willing to look for it. I'm very excited to see what's on the other side of this, even if I'm not very enthused about the process of getting there.

We'll get through this together... now let's get going.

Jeff Bajorek
April 2020

# P.A.R.E. THINGS DOWN

CHAPTER
1

# P.A.R.E. Things Down

I was talking to a sales leader recently, and she summed it up perfectly... "When it gets hard out there, you have to keep things simple."

When it feels like it's hitting the fan, you need to stop what you're doing and identify what's really important. You need to PARE things down. I certainly don't make a living coming up with acronyms, but this one presented itself. This is how my little acronym breaks down...

*P*ause

*A*ssess

*R*eflect

*E*xecute

## PAUSE

The worst thing you can do in situations like this is panic (that's the wrong 'P'). As information and emotions swirl around you, you need to **Pause** and break those cycles to stop that madness. Take stock of your current physical state, and change it.

Put your phone down. Take a walk. Take a deep breath, or four...

If you're reading this right now, you're likely physically safe. Now that you've checked that box, give yourself the headspace to think clearly.

## ASSESS

Now you can shift your mindset, **Assess** your situation, and identify what needs to be done. Remind yourself what you know to be true. Just the facts. What got you into this situation? How much of it was under your control? Did you really do this to yourself, or is this an environment that everybody is dealing with? When you identify what got you here, it becomes a little clearer what will get you out.

Are you currently in a global pandemic that few even saw coming and nobody really knows how to react? Relax. You're not alone, and quite frankly, you're not responsible for having all of the answers.

Are you running into an issue where your lack of pipeline put a little too much pressure on that last deal that didn't go through, and now you're not going to hit your number? This is a different situation, but one in which you probably have some answers.

In any situation, even in those where it feels like there are a lot of things you can't do, there is almost always a list of things you can do that will positively impact your current state of affairs. Think about them and write them down.

Maybe it's a list you keep for yourself with pen and paper. Maybe it's a whiteboard exercise that you do with your team. Maybe you're working remotely and need to connect virtually through a cloud-based document or a video call.

Regardless of the medium, forward-thinking, constructive activities like these build positive energy and momentum. You feel like progress is being made because you're focusing on what can be done instead of what can't be done. Lists like these are energizing because they highlight what you can control. You recognize the things that will make a difference, and you feel you can actually act on them.

### REFLECT

Now that you have your list, identify and prioritize the top three things on it. A few pages ago, I asked you to think about what led to this situation, what you did to cause it, what you didn't, and what you can do to help get out of it. *Reflect* on your best next steps. It might be difficult to decide. If that's the case, then you probably have a lot of great options. You don't have to ignore the rest, but you do need to set them aside for a bit while you work on the top three.

Inevitably, your focused execution of these top three initiatives (in order of importance) will eliminate the need for a lot of the other options further down the line. This is actually how you know you're working on the right things. Trust the process.

While you're in your planning stage, ask yourself...

* What needs to be done?

* Who needs to be involved?

* How can we best accomplish these things?

The answers to these questions help you formulate your plan. Write it down and put it where you can see it (perhaps that whiteboard where everybody can see it). Not only will this help you effectively communicate your plan, but just writing it down will help to ingrain the purpose and the steps in your mind.

## EXECUTE

The most important step, as always, is to **Execute** that plan. This may be easier said than done, but you've gone through the difficult process of identifying the most important tasks and planned the best way to go about performing them. Now it's time for you to act.

You've done the hard work necessary to make the implementation as easy as it can be. Don't turn back, and do not get distracted. You can't afford to.

This is actually a tremendous opportunity to differentiate yourself and be seen as a leader. Whether it's a crisis that affects us all, or it's one that you inadvertently created for yourself, your customers want to be led. You are capable of that leadership. In fact, you signed up for it. Lean in now and move forward. Others will not be so bold as to take the steps you've already taken. Take advantage of this new opportunity and focus on what needs to be done.

# WHAT YOU CAN DO

## CHAPTER
### 2

# *What You Can Do*

I n times of crisis, it's understandable to think about the things you cannot do, but I think that's the wrong lens through which to look at things. Worrying about things you cannot control is an unproductive mindset.

Instead of sitting in anger, disappointment, frustration, or fear at the thought of what you cannot do, why not stop and think about whether or not those things are important?

Maybe focusing too much on things outside of your control contributed to your dip in the first place...

You're faced with foreboding circumstances. You only have so much capacity, and you cannot afford to take anything for granted. Start taking inventory... What's really important?

Once you have your priorities identified and have ruled out some of the things you probably shouldn't be doing, think about what you can do within those new boundaries..

## LOOK AT WHAT'S POSSIBLE, AND START WITH THE BASICS.

Take control of your schedule. Start by eliminating everything on your calendar that isn't one of your top three priorities. Then start to fill that empty space with work that will help tackle those priorities. Determine what's essential to your goals and really scrutinize everything else.

Recognize that you can be remarkably productive in a short amount of time if you have a little bit of discipline and allow yourself the space to focus. You don't have to fill every slot in your calendar. In fact I don't advise it. It's very difficult to do your very best work when you're booked back-to-back all day. Your ideas and your ability to execute require space.

Sharpen your message. Revisit the first two of *The Five Forgotten Fundamentals of Prospecting*.

1. **Know what you bring to the table**

   * Why are you different?

   * Why are you valuable?

   * Why does that matter?

2. **Know who you should be talking to**

- Who are they?

- Why they would buy from you?

- Why wouldn't they?

Reach out and make human connections. During a global crisis, understand that the value you thought you brought even a week or two ago may not be the value your prospects need from you right now. If you find yourself in a more typical rut, you may be pressing and developing some bad habits. Either way, revisit your approach.

Instead of asking yourself, "What can I sell my prospects today?" Ask, "What do my prospects need from me today?" There's a simple, yet profound mindset shift there. Establish yourself as someone worth talking to with something worth talking about. Give your prospects and customers a good reason to speak with you and you'll start to dig yourself out of this hole.

Need some specific action items? I've got some suggestions for you...

- Time block like crazy; set aside time to do your most important tasks, and hold yourself accountable to those boundaries

- Re-evaluate your sales process; look for gaps and think of ways to fill them

- Connect your similar customers and prospects by leading a small group that helps them tackle their business challenges

- Send thank you notes to your best customers

- Ask your best customers why they bought from you the first time, and why they continue to buy from you

- Get an old colleague on the phone and talk through your situation

## ALL YOU CAN DO

There's always more that can be done. Take a look at social media, and you'll feel as if there's always someone doing more than you. Doing more is not valuable though, if the activities aren't worth doing. Resist the urge to be busy for the sake of being busy.

I was raised to not "stand there with my hands in my pockets" and to "hurry every chance you get." Sound advice in general, but it can lead to a desire to act when no action is necessary. Sometimes all you can do is really all you can do, and trying to do more just means digging a deeper hole.

You've already done the work to decide what is important and worth doing. Set a boundary around what is enough and keep it. Yes, you will still have more time in the day, and you should. This is the time you spend with all of the things you're working so hard for- your family, your friends, your hobbies... If you don't get to enjoy those things, why are you working so hard? Are you working to live or living to work? You can't afford to lose this perspective.

## CROSS TRAINING FOR YOUR BRAIN

When you've done all you can for now, it's time to move on to something else. That might mean reading a novel or watching the game on tv. It might mean going on a date with your spouse or to the playground with your kids.

Stephen Covey wrote about sharpening the saw. A tool that is not properly maintained will eventually break- and some will break sooner than others. It's important to realize that you have limits, and that the concept of continuous improvement does not mean immediate perfection.

This isn't necessarily kicking back and putting your feet up though. In a lot of ways, taking a break from work can serve as cross training for your mind. There are a lot of ways you can stay mentally challenged and engaged without the grind. Here are just a few...

- Learn to cook

- Plant a vegetable garden

- Invest in yourself with the wealth of resources available online

- Reach out and connect with an old roommate or friend

- Teach your kids something, use stories from when you grew up

- Tackle a project around the house, particularly one you're not sure how to do

- Start writing

- Read a book (nonfiction); not just guides for how to sell better, but learn from the experiences and perspectives of others- their processes, journeys, and life lessons

- Read a book (fiction); great stories remind us of our own journeys and the twists and turns they take

- Dream big about something

- Take a deep breath (repeat)

## THERE IS POWER IN CONNECTING WITH OTHER PEOPLE

Whenever I mentally engage in conversations with other people about what is possible rather than what isn't, I leave the conversation energized and ready to do something. On the contrary, if I allow myself to mire in the current less-than-ideal situation, I feel like distracting myself and doing something less than productive.

Escapism is not a solution.

Pick up the phone. Call a colleague, a friend, an old roommate... someone with a positive outlook and a different perspective. Some of the best connections you can make happen during uncertain times. The conversations you have may be just enough to shift your point of view, and that can make all the difference.

# WHAT'S REALLY IMPORTANT

**CHAPTER**

3

# What's Really Important

Y ou learn a lot in times of crisis. When everything goes sideways, you re-evaluate what's really important. Here are a few things our current situation has taught me.

- There have been a lot of meetings that could have been memos

- There have been a lot of memos that probably didn't need to be sent

- There were a lot of 800-word blog posts that should have been 400

- There were a lot of things on your calendar that may have felt like sales activities, but weren't really helping to accomplish many sales

In other words, you probably weren't being very intentional, and were doing a lot of things just for the optics.

When things go sideways, the non-essential stuff needs to go out the window. The intention behind PARE is to identify what's really important, set boundaries around those things, and execute them first.

*Well, when you put it that way, shouldn't that be how we always go about doing things?*

Bingo.

## MEASURE WHAT MATTERS

You've seen the people at the gym who are really only there so they can be known as someone who goes to the gym. You know people in your company who often show up early and leave late. You also know people on your sales team whose data hygiene is sparkling, and their CRM is up to date to the minute.

These people want you to believe that they care, and that they're good at what they do. To the naked eye, that may be exactly what it looks like.

Still, I see people at my gym who are there almost every time I am, but barely break a sweat. Just because that person shows up before anyone else and occasionally stays late doesn't mean they do better (or even more) work than you do. Don't get me wrong, data entry is important, but can you please help me understand why being so thorough about telling me what you did is going to help you do more of it tomorrow?

Plausible deniability (that's a great phase isn't it?), covers up a lot of mediocrity. Too many sellers are out there trying to make it look like they're doing great work in order to cover up for the fact that they're really not. Working hard to make it look like you're working hard doesn't make sense to me. I think it's actually less work to deliver results if you apply the right focus.

## WHAT MATTERS TO YOU?

At the end of the day, there are only two things you can do that will help you sell more.

1. Spend more active time in your sales process

2. Make sure that you're asking for appropriate next steps within that process

That's it. Every other problem that you and your team run into is a derivative of one of those two issues. Either you're not spending enough time in front of your customers selling, or you're not advancing the process with those customers.

Ask your average salesperson how much time they've spent in each of the past three weeks interacting with customers, and if they could tell you how much, they'd be embarrassed to say it out loud.

It will never cease to amaze me how professional salespeople, *who in many cases only get paid when someone commits to a sale,* refuse to nudge their prospects to even get closer to doing so.

Wanna get your territory back on track? Make those two metrics the only ones you measure.

## WHAT MATTERS TO YOUR PROSPECTS AND CUSTOMERS?

This one is a little more nuanced, but if you're going to spend more time with your customers in your sales process, and you're going to be consistently moving forward, you need to be able to answer this question.

In times of crisis, a CEO could be concerned about the safety of the business. It could be about making sure that she makes payroll next period or doesn't default on that loan payment.

In better times, that same CEO may have a lot of options on her plate and wonders which is the best next step to take. The paradox of choice can be debilitating. In the presence of several options for taking her business to the next level, it's typically the one with the highest potential reward and the lowest perceived amount of risk that's going to win out.

A mid-level executive is almost always thinking about how their decision will make them look, and whether or not a bad one will get them fired- the optics again.

You see the theme of risk running pretty consistently throughout your buyer's concerns, so it's important to think about how your demeanor and selling style is either calming or inflaming that sense of risk. In other words, do they trust you to help them take that next step?

So, I'll ask again... Are you known as someone worth talking to and do you have something worth talking about?

Not coincidentally, that kind of reputation covers the entire sweet spot of what's important to you and what's important to your customers. People take your calls and agree to meet with you because they see the value in it. As a result, you get to spend more time actively selling, and have earned the opportunity to ask for next steps. The ability to execute those activities has never been more valuable.

# WHAT'S IMPORTANT NOW IS ALWAYS IMPORTANT

# What's Important Now Is Always Important

I t wasn't that long ago when the economy felt like it was riding high. People were in a good mood. Many businesses, though some certainly had their challenges, were growing. The stock market was trading at what seemed like a new all-time high every day.

Maybe you're coming off your best year ever. Maybe you've taken on a new position or been promoted. You're in a really good emotional place, and everything's coming up roses...

All of a sudden, things are less certain.

## IT'S EASIER TO SELL IN TIMES OF ABUNDANCE

When things are good, it's easy to get a little sloppy with your technique. With a wider margin for error, your skills don't need to be as sharp. A lot of mediocrity can be disguised as success.

You're not the only one with a wider margin for error. When your customers perceive less risk, they're more open to new ideas and are more willing to be creative. They're also willing to spend more money with more people.

But then it hits the fan...

Now all of a sudden, people don't know what to do or how to feel. When things aren't so good, people hold onto their money. They circle the wagons and have a much narrower perspective.

Decision-making processes get delayed, or even shut down indefinitely. The perception of risk goes through the roof, even when the decision to move forward with your solution was a no-brainer a week ago.

With fewer resources, now there's more perceived competition than ever before. You're not just up against the competition in your space, but your customers and clients are deciding which decisions they're even going to move forward with.

My, how things change...

## TIGHTEN UP

Now, more than ever, you need to tighten up. Your mindset, your skillset, your process... all of them. You need to be at your best, because nothing less than that will suffice.

The funny thing is, you really don't need to call in special forces or adopt a radical new technique or solution. You just need to execute on the fundamentals you've likely forgotten or ignored. When things are good, you can get away with getting a little loose. When things aren't so good, you need to be on your best behavior.

Reinvest in your routine. Get up at the same time every day. Time block your most important activities both for work and for you. That means blocks for prospecting, meetings, and follow-up, as well as exercise, family time, and quiet time to be still and think.

It's worth noting, that even when you feel like there's a lot on your plate, if you just list all the things you want to do during a day, you realize there's almost always time for all of them.

Revisit your messaging to your ideal customers. Engage with them regularly. Prioritize meaningful interactions that deepen your connection. Now is the time to provide more value for your customers, not selfishly check in to see if they've made a decision yet.

Shouldn't you be doing this regularly anyway? Maybe your marketing department came up with the message, but your delivery is a crucial component in its effectiveness. Are you hitting the right notes? What are your colleagues doing that's working for them?

I want to be clear on something. Even when it goes sideways, you are still playing a long game. I'll double down and say it's the only game you should ever be playing.

When you PARE things down, remember that the 'P' stands for 'Pause' not 'Panic.' You're doubling your long-term efforts and execution on the fundamentals, not cutting your price in half. Now is not the time to appear desperate and try to "wheel and deal" your way into some revenue. All that will accomplish is damaging both your personal brand and your company's. What you sell shouldn't be worth less just because you're in a hurry.

Do the right things for the right reasons. Then keep doing them.

For a sales rep in the field, that might mean not pulling ahead orders from May to make up for a shortfall in April. For a sales leader, that means having a long-term vision for the team and staying the course, and not being so reactive to the relatively small bumps in the road along the way.

You see, whether you're in the midst of a personal sales slump or a global pandemic, the activities that will get you out of trouble now are the same ones that will keep you out of trouble later.

I'll go back to time spent selling and advancing sales processes as the only two metrics that really matter. When I work with and study top performers, that's what they focus on. Every other activity in their routine supports those two objectives.

This is your opportunity to revisit your own routine and make the necessary adjustments so that you can say the same.

# HIT THE RESET BUTTON

**CHAPTER**

5

# Hit The Reset Button

**C**risis reveals character. It also presents opportunity.

When it all goes sideways, you have the opportunity to recognize what's really important, and you get a different look at things...

## TRIM THE FAT

Were there things you were doing before that you don't need to do anymore? Perhaps there were workflows, automations, or campaigns that weren't getting the job done, but you felt you were just too busy to dig into them?

Maybe you knew you had some bad habits that weren't productive, but it would have been too painful to go through the transition to something better?

Right now, given the elimination of everything that is non-essential in your process, you have the time to give things a good, hard look. You owe it to yourself to do so, because the health and success of your business going forward are dependent on it.

## A FRESH START

There are two specific times in my life where I remember fresh starts being huge catalysts in my life. The first was switching schools between the 6th and 7th grades. Every twelve-year-old deserves a reset button, but that's another topic for another time.

The second, and more significant time was when I left my first sales job to take a new one. Over the previous three years, I had done a lot of self-study, had found a great mentor, and laid the foundation for my own selling style.

There were a lot of things I thought I needed to do differently in order to be really effective, but it still seemed too daunting of a task to uproot my current processes and routines and make the changes.

I was scared. Everything in my job already felt fragile, and making changes felt risky. Couldn't I just execute better in my current systems? I didn't realize what I was missing.

I ended up getting the right call from the right recruiter on the right day, and I made the leap. This new environment gave me the opportunity to implement some new habits. If it turned out that what felt right to me was not actually an effective way to sell, then maybe I just wasn't cut out for a sales gig after all.

What felt right to me meant focusing on executing within a sales process instead of doing the facetious things that salespeople do. It turns out that all the face time in the world doesn't mean much unless you're having productive conversations...

Sound familiar?

It didn't take long for me to realize that my instincts were correct. The changes I wanted to implement felt right, and they worked.

Thinking about it over a decade later, this is really where my *Rethink The Way You Sell* philosophy started to grow into something. I had an opportunity to rid myself of the assumptions I had been making about how to sell, and I started to replace those actions with some that made more sense to me.

Within 18 months, I had tripled the revenue in my territory while working about a third of the hours. The simple math on that is a 9X increase in productivity, all because I had the guts to do the right work instead of worrying about looking like I was doing a lot of work.

In hindsight, my first sales job wasn't a great fit, but I didn't need to get a new job in order to rethink the way I was selling and make changes. I just used that reset as my opportunity to go all in. Your current slump may be just enough of an opportunity for you to do the same.

## HOW WILL YOU RESPOND?

The coronavirus pandemic has changed a lot of careers. For some people, it may mean they're looking for a new job. In some ways, the job you currently have may just feel like a new job. Regardless, there are opportunities to really optimize the way you work, and I think they will optimize the results you get.

What will you do differently that will help get you out of this situation? What do your clients and customers need from you right now?

Do you need to pivot to a new product offering? Is there some new technology that can help you respond to the changing needs of your customers? Or do you just need to hunker down, tighten up, and move forward?

Use this opportunity to think about the next right thing to do with the people you serve in mind. That intention, along with a renewed focus on your fundamentals, will make your business much more sustainable now and into the future.

# KEEP YOUR SWAGGER

**CHAPTER**

6

# Keep Your Swagger

I never told you selling was going to be easy, and anybody who did was either horribly misinformed or outright lying to you. Before you get too disappointed, let me make sure your expectations are appropriately managed.

Spring of 2020 brought the first global pandemic of any of our professional lifetimes. For a lot of you reading this who have only been selling for a few years, it's entirely possible that this is the first time you've seen any market-wide downturn or instability.

While this may be your first slump, valley, trough, or whatever you'd like to call it, it will certainly not be the last one you face. I seemed to run into at least one or two mini slumps every year when I was out on the field.

Typically, the solution was pretty simple- and PARE was enough of a reset to do the trick. The hardest part was always that first 'P- Pause.' It's really hard to pause when things get out of control, but that's actually the point.

When things feel out of control, it's typically because you're trying to wrangle things that can't be wrangled. When you refocus your efforts toward things you can actually influence, you're much more effective, and you feel better almost immediately.

Once I Paused, it was a lot easier to Assess, Reflect, and Execute. I suspect the same will be true for you if you let yourself. If you really need it, consider this permission from me to do so.

## YOU'RE THE BEST IN THE WORLD

Remind yourself what you know to be true, and go back to a phrase I've been reminding you to tell yourself every morning for the past couple of years...

*I'm the best in the world at what I do, and the really scary part is that I'm only half as good as I'm going to be.*

This phrase is *always* true. When you recognize that, you feel a little better. When you say it to yourself in the mirror 100 times before you get to work each day, you're ready to run through brick walls for what you believe in. If you've read this far, my guess is that you could really use that kind of mindset right now.

## YOU WILL GET THROUGH THIS, AND YOU
## WILL BE BETTER FOR IT

One of the reasons I enjoy reading biographies is that I get to recognize how difficult it is for even the most successful people. Adversity breeds toughness, resiliency and creativity; and that's exactly what you need to dig yourself out of these situations.

Essentially, it's times like these that bring out our very best.

Remember, this too shall pass. Brighter days are coming, and smoother sailing is ahead. I promise. Peaks and valleys are a part of life. How you approach the spaces between the peaks dictates how big those spaces are.

Look a little closer... Do you realize that the peaks get higher as you progress? Notice that the valleys aren't quite as low either. With all of the emphasis on forward progress, it's easy to forget that the best way to measure your growth isn't how close you are to the summit, but how far you've climbed since the beginning.

My first sales manager told me not to "get too high with the highs or too low with the lows." Sure, that sounds great and all, but I didn't have a ton of context for that until much later in my career.

I take the concept and spin it a little differently. I say that when you focus on process, you get results. But when you focus on results, you get frustrated. Get back to the things you know you can control, your mindset and your actions, and set the course. Do the things you know will produce results, spend time in front of customers and advance those processes. The results will come in time. While they never seem to come fast enough, they always come as fast as they can.

## TWISTS AND TURNS

There's a labyrinth in the woods at Bandon Dunes Golf Resort- one of my favorite places on the planet. It's designed for walking meditation and is a replica of one on the floor in a cathedral in Chartres, France.

This is the inscription on the plaque right before you enter it.

*"The labyrinth is a metaphor for our journey through life. Its path leads toward an inner light, to the center of our self and the center of the sacred; one and the same.*

*It's direction, at times, is confusing, taking us around, and then back again. Yet, it is through this circular journey of discovery and growth that we reconnect to where we once began."*

I've walked in that labyrinth. I've meditated in that labyrinth. I've cried in that labyrinth. It's a perfect metaphor for the inexplicable twists and turns our lives take. Sometimes the only comfort we can take is knowing that those twists and turns were meant to teach us something about a lesson that's bigger than we can appreciate in the moment. But if we can keep moving forward, then someday (hopefully soon), we'll be able to fully appreciate those lessons.

## KEEP TAKING STEPS

Sometimes progress feels like moving in quicksand. Other times, you feel like you're running a four-minute mile. Try not to get caught up in what it feels like and turn your focus instead on continuing to move forward.

No step is too small if it's headed in the right direction. What's important is that you keep taking steps.

You know what you need to do right now. In almost every case, as you've learned thus far, they're the things you should have been doing all along, and you should keep doing forever. Stop worrying about what will happen and how much (the results), and get to work (your process).

LIFE GOES ON

CHAPTER

7

# Life Goes On

Y ou may be struggling right now. You may be thinking (even aloud) that if this too shall pass, then when? What I know from experience is that in order to make the most progress coming out of a situation like this, you need to be as present and mindful as possible through it.

As much as you may want to take a nap for two weeks and wake up when it's all over, I'm afraid that would not deliver the results you're looking for. Be here, experience it. Live through it, don't sleepwalk past it. You need to confront this discomfort in order to truly benefit from what lies on the other side, which is a stronger, more thoughtful and resilient version of your current self..

## IN THE BLINK OF AN EYE

Ever get away for a weekend and leave the kids at home, only to return and feel like they've aged 6 months while you were gone? It's amazing what a few days away can do, let alone a winter between bike rides.

I took one of those spring bike rides with my son on a recent Monday evening. It was a little chilly, but still warm enough to get out after dinner. It was our first ride together of the spring, and we had some pent-up energy to release.

Buster remembered all the rules, and even reminded me of a few of them. He was paying attention to traffic and intersections, even some things I had forgotten I had taught him about staying safe. Who was this kid?

Since the start of the school year, my daughter has gone up two shoe sizes, and none of her pajamas fit her anymore. She's having a hard time letting go of them, which indicates to me that things may even be moving a little quickly for her taste as well.

I'm not the kind of parent that writes sappy social media posts about "where has the time gone?" But I did notice something... Time does not stand still because you are in a crisis. If you don't stop to pay attention to what's going on around you, you're going to miss it, and you never get this time back.

Times like these remind me that regardless of what's going on in the world, there are still lessons to be learned, people to connect with and lead, and yes, even sales to be made.

My kids are only going to be this age once, and what's more important than my work, my clients, even my career, is that I'm the best dad I can be to them. You cannot let the less important things in life take precedence over the stuff that really matters.

Life goes on, whether you like it or not. Learn from your experiences, and then apply those lessons in the future.

Keep moving forward. Keep learning. Keep living.

## ARE YOU LOOKING TO MAKE THINGS GO FORWARD INSTEAD OF SIDEWAYS?

### I CAN HELP.

Let's have a conversation about what you're facing and why you feel stuck. Send an email to jb@jeffbajorek.com, and let's schedule some time to talk. We'll come up with some ideas and next steps to get your business headed in the right direction again.

# *Acknowledgments*

T his project just clicked. What was on my mind was what people needed (and told me they wanted) to hear. Still, there is no way I could have done this without a strong team who helped bring it to life in short order:

Liz Borchert's brilliant design work. Laurel Sutherland and Paula Bajorek's thoughtful editing eyes. My trusted peers' generosity to review, validate, and challenge this piece: I'm looking at Mike Simmons, Camille Clemons, David Weiss, Andy Racic, Mike Weinberg, Jacquelyn Nicholson, Alex Smith, and Nick Fawle. And those who routinely inspire me: Christie Walters, Vince Fowler, Liz Wendling, Larry Levine, Jason Bay, and Don The Idea Guy Holliday.

Of course, none of this would be possible without the love and support of my family, who somehow didn't mind that I disappeared for a week during quarantine to work on this project.

It takes a village, and what a village!

Thank you,

*JB*

# NOTES:

# NOTES:

# NOTES:

Made in the USA
Monee, IL
15 July 2020